Dance

Bollywood Dance

By Trudy Becker

level 2
little blue readers

www.littlebluehousebooks.com

Little Blue House is distributed by North Star Editions:
sales@northstareditions.com | 888-417-0195

Produced for Little Blue House by Red Line Editorial.

Photographs ©: iStockphoto, cover, 15, 16, 24 (top left), 24 (bottom left); Shutterstock Images, 4, 9, 10, 13, 19, 21, 23, 24 (top right), 24 (bottom right); Pexels, 7

Library of Congress Control Number: 2022920069

ISBN
978-1-64619-828-3 (hardcover)
978-1-64619-857-3 (paperback)
978-1-64619-912-9 (ebook pdf)
978-1-64619-886-3 (hosted ebook)

Printed in the United States of America
Mankato, MN
082023

About the Author

Trudy Becker lives in Minneapolis, Minnesota. She likes exploring new places and loves anything involving books.

Table of Contents

jewelry

Moving Colors

Many kids dance together.
They wear colorful clothes
and jewelry.
They move their arms
and spin.

A girl's beautiful clothes flow. Bangles make a jingling sound when she moves.

bangles

A dancing boy moves his hands in different poses.

He lifts his foot.

He is doing Bollywood dance.

All About It

Bollywood dance comes
from India.
It is used in movies.
It has many kinds of moves.

Some moves started
in India.
Some come from
other places.
When they are mixed, it
makes Bollywood dance.

Dancers tell stories with their bodies.
They often use hand positions.
Each position means something different.

hand position

Learning How

Bollywood dancers practice before shows. They have to work together. If they practice hard, the whole group can do well.

They learn all the moves.
Sometimes they practice
in a class.
Other times they practice
at home.

When dancers perform, they wear bright outfits. They shine and jingle. Fancy outfits help dancers tell a story and look beautiful.

outfit

Before showtime, dancers stretch out their arms, legs, and necks.
They fix their jewelry.
It is time for Bollywood dance!

Glossary

bangles

jewelry

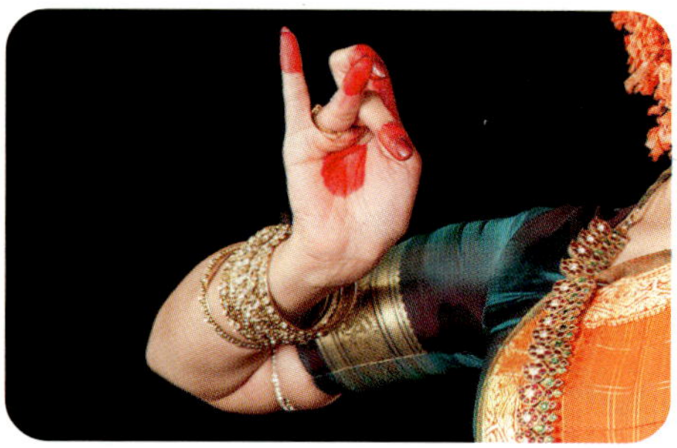

hand position

outfit

Index